Working as a Team

Guided/Group Reading Notes

White Band

Contents

OXFORD

Introduction

Reading progression in Year 2/Primary 3

In Year 2/P3 children begin to read longer, more challenging and less familiar texts independently. Most children are able to decode new words quickly and automatically, and this helps them build up their pace, fluency and stamina.

The Project X texts at **white band** are slightly longer than those at gold band but still contain a core of familiar high and medium frequency words and phonically regular words to help build children's confidence as they become independent readers.

The range of genre and writing styles continues to expand. A storyline or theme may be sustained over a longer period of time and simple 'non-chronological' plots will be introduced with clear pointers for the reader about changes in or passage of time. More sophisticated fantasy elements such as time travel are introduced.

The characters continue to develop in complexity and more than one point of view is expressed within the text. Information or action is increasingly implied rather than spelled out. Sentence structure will be longer and more subordinate phrases or clauses are included. Similes and metaphors, as well as technical language where appropriate, are used. Examples of 'literary' language are frequent.

A range of non-fiction features including charts, maps, tables, labelled diagrams, captions, indexes and glossaries are used to encourage children to read and interpret information presented in a variety of ways.

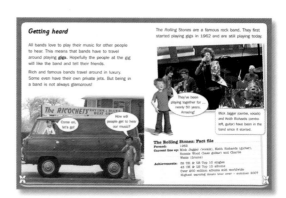

2

Visual literacy is supported through additional action and information in the illustrations, the use of graphic devices and cartoon and comic-strip genres and the suggestions for visualization comprehension strategies suggested in these notes.

Progression in the Project X character books

In this cluster, we explore how the characters work as a team. We also meet some more red X-bots and find out that they are not all as nice as Ant's pet robot, Rover. In *The Balloon Team*, the children make a micro balloon – but things get a little scary when they decide to go for a ride. They have to work together to get themselves safely back down to the ground. In *Divided We Fall*, Cat, Ant and Tiger leave Max to clean the micro-buggy by himself. They soon realize they need his help when some red X-bots turn up and try to steal Tiger's watch! Questions are left open as to what X-bots really are, where they come from and why they were trying to get the watches.

These two stories help to add a layer of intrigue with regards to the overall series plot and will encourage readers to want to know more about the X-bots. It also shows that someone is after the watches. Links can be made to earlier books in the series: *The Thing in the Cupboard* (Communication) and *Message in an X-bot* (Communication).

Guided/group reading

The engaging content and careful levelling of the Project X books makes them ideal for use in guided/group reading sessions. The advantages of using guided/group reading, as well as charts to help you assess the appropriate level for a reading group, are discussed in the *Teaching Handbook* for Year 2/P3.

To use the books in guided/group reading sessions, you should select a book at a band that creates a small degree of challenge for the group of pupils. Typically, children should be able to read about 90% of the book unaided. This level of 'readability' provides the context for children to practise their reading and build reading confidence. The 'challenge' in the text provides opportunities for explicitly teaching reading skills.

These *Guided/Group Reading Notes* provide support for each book in the cluster, along with suggestions for follow-up activities. Books in the white band can be covered in one or two reading sessions. Alternatively, children may read much of each book independently.

Speaking, listening and drama

Talk is crucial to learning. Children need plenty of opportunities to express their ideas through talk and drama, and to listen to and watch the ideas of others. These processes are important for building reading engagement, personal response and understanding. Suggestions for speaking, listening and drama are given for every book. Within these *Guided/Group Reading Notes* the speaking and listening activities are linked to the reading assessment focuses.

Building comprehension

Understanding what we have read is at the heart of reading. To help readers become effective in comprehending a text these *Guided/Group Reading Notes* contain practical strategies to develop the following important aspects of comprehension:

- Previewing
- Predicting
- Activating and building prior knowledge
- Questioning
- Recalling
- Visualizing and other sensory responses
- Deducing, inferring and drawing conclusions
- Determining importance
- Synthesizing
- Empathizing
- Summarizing
- Personal response, including adopting a critical stance.

The research basis and rationale for focusing on these aspects of comprehension is given in the *Teaching Handbook* for Year 2/P3.

Reading fluency

Reading fluency combines automatic word recognition, reading with pace, and expression. Rereading, fluency and building comprehension support each other. This is discussed more fully in the *Teaching Handbook* for Year 2/P3. Opportunities for children to read aloud are important in building fluency and reading aloud to children provides models of expressive fluent reading. Suggestions for purposeful and enjoyable oral reading and rereading/re-listening activities are given in the follow-up activities to guided/group reading and in the notes for parents on the inside cover of each book.

The Project X *Interactive Stories* software can be used to provide a model of reading fluency for the whole class and/or opportunities for individuals or small groups of children to listen to stories again and again. Listening to stories being read is particularly effective with EAL children.

Building vocabulary

Explicit work on enriching vocabulary is important in building reading fluency and comprehension. Repeatedly encountering a word and its variants helps it become familiar and supports both reading and spelling. The thematic 'cluster' structure of Project X supports this because words are repeated within and across the books. Suggestions for vocabulary work are included in these notes. The vocabulary chart on pages 10 and 11 shows when vocabulary is repeated and new words are introduced. It also indicates those words that can be used to support learning alongside a structured phonics and spelling programme.

Developing a thematic approach

Helping children make links in their learning supports their development as learners. All the books in this cluster have a focus on the theme **Working as a Team**. A chart showing the cross-curricular potential of this theme is given in the *Teaching Handbook* for Year 2/P3, along with a rationale for using thematic approaches. Some suggestions for cross-curricular activities are also given in these notes, in the follow-up suggestions for each book.

In guided/group reading sessions, you will also want to encourage children to make links between the books in the cluster. Grouping books in a cluster allows readers to make links between characters, events and actions across the books. This enables readers to gradually build complex understandings of characters, to give reasons why things happen and how characters may change and develop. It can help them recognize cause and effect. It helps children reflect on the skill of determining importance, as a minor incident or detail in one book may prove to have greater significance when considered across several books.

Note that the character books in this cluster can be read in any order.

In the **Working as a Team** cluster, some of the suggested links that can be explored across the books include:

- working as a team to paint a picture (**Art and design**)
- team building activities (**PE, PSHE**)
- exploring examples of teamwork over the ages (**History**).

Reading into writing

The Project X books provide both models and inspiration to support children's writing. Suggestions for relevant, contextualized and interesting writing activities are given in the follow-up activities for each book. These include both short and longer writing opportunities. The activities cover a wide range of writing contexts so writers can develop an understanding of adapting their writing for different audiences and purposes.

The Project X *Interactive Stories* software contains a collection of 'clip art' assets from the characters books – characters, setting and props – that children can use in their writing.

There are also a number of writing frames that can be downloaded and printed for pupils to use, or that pupils can write/type into directly to practise writing and ICT skills.

Selecting follow-up activities

These *Guided/Group Reading Notes* give many ideas for follow-up activities. Some of these can be completed within the reading session. Some are longer activities that will need to be worked on over time. You should select those activities that are most appropriate for your pupils. It is not expected that you would complete all the suggested activities.

Home/school reading

Books used in a guided/group reading session can also be used in home/school reading programmes.

Before a guided/group reading session the child could:
- read the first chapter or section of a book
- read a related book from the cluster to build background knowledge.

Following a guided/group reading session, the child could:
- reread the book at home to build reading confidence and fluency
  - read the next chapter in a longer book
    - read a related book from the cluster.

      Advice for parents on supporting their child in reading at home is provided in the inside covers of individual books. There is further advice for teachers concerning home/school reading partnerships in the *Teaching Handbook* for Year 2/P3.

Assessment

During guided/group reading, teachers make ongoing assessments of individuals and of the group. Reading targets are indicated for each book and you should assess against them. You should select just one or two targets at a time as the focus for the group. The same target can be appropriate for several literacy sessions or over several texts.

Readers should be encouraged to self-assess and peer-assess against the target/s.

Further support for assessing pupils' progress is provided in the *Teaching Handbook* for Year 2/P3.

Continuous reading objectives and ongoing assessment

The following objectives will be supported in *every* guided/group reading session and are therefore a *continuous* focus for attention and assessment. These objectives are not listed in full for each book, but as you listen to individual children reading you should undertake ongoing assessment, against these decoding and encoding objectives:

- Read independently and with increasing fluency longer and less familiar texts **5.1**
- Know how to tackle unfamiliar words that are not completely decodable **5.3**
- Read and spell less common alternative graphemes including trigraphs **5.4**
- Read high and medium frequency words independently and automatically **5.5**

Further objectives are provided as a focus within the notes for each book. Correlation to the specific objectives within the Scottish, Welsh and Northern Irish curricula are provided in the *Teaching Handbook* for Year 2/P3.

 Recording assessment

The assessment chart for the **Working as a Team** cluster is provided on page 50 of the Teaching Handbook for Year 2/P3.

 Diagnostic assessment

If an individual child is failing to make good progress or he or she seems to have a specific problem with some aspect of reading you will want to undertake a more detailed assessment. Details of how to use running records for diagnostic assessment are given in the *Teaching Handbook* for Year 2/P3.

Vocabulary chart

At Year 2/P3, the children should:

- read high and medium frequency words independently and automatically
- read and spell
  - less common alternative graphemes
  - compound words and polysyllabic words
  - suffixes and prefixes.

NB There are too many high frequency words in each book to list them all. The first 100 words are known by this stage. A selection is given from the final 200 words in the *300 common words in order of frequency* list. Examples only are given in each category.

The Balloon Team	High frequency words	began, morning, everyone, room
	Phonetically regular compound and polysyllabic words	splendid, garden, hooted, swooping, scattering, hissed, tilted, glittering
	Alternative graphemes including trigraphs	steer, sight, suggested, technology, assured, serious, climbed, sigh, voice, horrified, dangerously, colourful, kite, squawking, strained, surrounded, alright, cloud, tied, weight, building, direction, heading
	Challenge words	idea, technology, serious, direction, concentrated, weight
Divided We Fall	High frequency words	friends, shouted, something, again
	Phonetically regular compound and polysyllabic words	bleeped, buckets, reluctantly, finished, himself, adventure
	Alternative graphemes including trigraphs	adventures, complained, clogged, sarcastically, accident, luckily, ducked, underneath, furious, reluctantly, concentrating, appeared, wicked, surrounded, skidded, scuttling, explanations, revved, engine, zoomed, splattered
	Challenge words	furious, climbed, sarcastically, decided, sponge, pincers

Let's Form a Band	High frequency words	only, who, lots, way, each, even
	Phonetically regular compound and polysyllabic words	together, fantastic, extra, layers, Internet, cartoon, charity, however
	Alternative graphemes including trigraphs	musician, guitarist, harmony, rhythm, sometimes, famous, record, audition, massive, include, produces, engineer, equipment, successful, except
	Challenge words	musician, guitarist, audition, rhythm, choreographer, songwriting
Fee Fie Fo... MUM!	High frequency words	going, other, stopped, began
	Phonetically regular compound and polysyllabic words	humming, yelled, cameras, waddling, wobble, blushing, cornflakes, beanstalk
	Alternative graphemes including trigraphs	alike, arguing, upstairs, shrieked, roared, dialled, speaking, wrote, dreams, scowling, voice, enormous, reflection, carefully, disappeared, whispered, quarrelling
	Challenge words	anxiously, scenery, excited, laughed
The Beautiful Team	High frequency words	over, know, next, great, first
	Phonetically regular compound and polysyllabic words	perform, brilliant, deformed, nickname, togetherness, attacking
	Alternative graphemes including trigraphs	position, referee, spine, stadium, substitute, train, coach, brilliant, suffer, certain, injured, season, receive
	Challenge words	Argentina, Jose Batista, Cafu, Carlos Alberto, Czechoslovakia, Vicente Feola, Garrincha, Liverpool, Ronaldhino, South America, Sweden, Uruguay, midfielders, beautiful, certain, experienced

The Balloon Team

BY CHRIS POWLING

About this book

The children decide to make a micro-hot-air balloon. They go on a flight, but end up being nearly caught in a kite, being swooped by birds and narrowly missing a building. With a bit of teamwork, the children manage to land the balloon safely.

You will need

- *Balloon words* Photocopy Master 60, *Teaching Handbook* for Year 2/P3
- *Balloon sound poem* Photocopy Master 61, *Teaching Handbook* for Year 2/P3
- Materials for making hot-air balloons (optional)
- Balloons! (optional)

	Literacy Framework objective	Target and assessment focus
Speaking, listening, group interaction and drama	○ Adopt appropriate roles in small or large groups and consider alternative courses of action **4.1**	○ We can take part in a group and think about how characters might behave **AF3**
Reading See also continuous reading objectives listed on page 9.	○ Explain their reactions to texts, commenting on important aspects **8.3** ○ Explore how particular words are used, including words and expressions with similar meanings **7.5**	○ We can explain our reactions to texts **AF6** ○ We can talk about how the writer has used words and how they imply characters' feelings **AF5**

Before reading

To activate prior knowledge and encourage prediction

- Discuss hot-air balloons with the children. What do they understand about how they fly? Have they ever seen a hot-air balloon? (**activating prior knowledge**)

- Turn to page 3 and read the paragraph that describes how hot-air balloons fly. Do the children know what an air current is? Take them outside and watch how things move in the wind, discuss wind direction and the erratic nature of the wind. Having looked at the nature of wind, talk to the children about what might happen in this story. (**predicting**)

To support decoding and introduce new vocabulary

- Look at the picture on pages 4–5. Encourage the children to write vocabulary to describe the scene on sticky notes and add them to the page. Alternatively, use the balloon shape provided on the *Balloon words* Photocopy Master and ask children to place the vocabulary on the page in the most appropriate place, e.g. pilot in the basket, etc. Children can add additional vocabulary.

- You may also wish to point out some of the high or medium frequency words or practise decoding some of the more challenging words in this book using the vocabulary chart on page 10.

To engage readers and support fluent reading

- Read Chapters 1 and 2 to the children. As you read, model how to use your voice to build excitement and tension.

During reading

- Ask the children to read Chapters 3 to 5.
- If you have not already done so, ask them what to do if they encounter a difficult word, modelling with an example from the book if necessary. Remind them of the more challenging vocabulary which you looked at before reading the book.
- As they read ask them to notice how the children are talking, especially Ant.

· >

 After reading

Returning to the text

- Ask the children to summarize what happened in the chapters. (**recall, summarizing**)
- Ask the children:
  - Do you think the characters worked well as a team together?
  - What happened when they let out more air from the balloon?
  - How did they manage to come back down to the ground? (**questioning**)

Building comprehension

- Do the children notice how the author used dialogue to show how Ant was feeling about going into the balloon? Why do they think Ant was not keen to get into the balloon? (**deducing, inferring, drawing conclusions**)

· >

- Allow the children to reflect on the story. Was it a good story? Which parts of the story did they enjoy and why? Are there any sections that they think could have been different? (**determining importance, personal response, adopting a critical stance**)

······························>

Building fluency

- Ask children to re-enact the scene when Ant tells the children that they do not have all the things they need to fly the balloon (Chapter 4). Ask them to think carefully about how they would feel. (**empathizing, personal response**)

- Encourage children to reflect on how they could have reacted differently, e.g. perhaps they would have been angry with Ant? (**adopting a critical stance**)

······························>

Building vocabulary

- Ask children to revisit the picture from pages 4 and 5 and take them outside to look at the sky and the wind. Now ask them to think of a word that best describes a balloon flight and write it on a (blown-up) balloon. Display the word balloons so they reach the ceiling of the room.

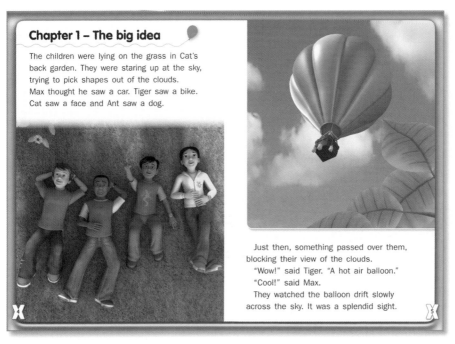

Chapter 1 – The big idea

The children were lying on the grass in Cat's back garden. They were staring up at the sky, trying to pick shapes out of the clouds.
Max thought he saw a car. Tiger saw a bike. Cat saw a face and Ant saw a dog.

Just then, something passed over them, blocking their view of the clouds.
"Wow!" said Tiger. "A hot air balloon."
"Cool!" said Max.
They watched the balloon drift slowly across the sky. It was a splendid sight.

Follow-up activities

Writing activities

- Write instructions for making a hot-air balloon. (**longer writing task**)
- Write an alternative adventure in the balloon. (**longer writing task**)
- Use the *Balloon sound poem* Photocopy Master to write a sound poem about being in a hot-air balloon. (**short writing task**)

Other literacy activities

- Children could role-play the scene in Chapter 5 when the characters take off in the balloon. (**drama**)

Cross-curricular and thematic opportunities

- Make hot-air balloons. See: http://pbskids.org/zoom/activities/sci/hotairballoon.html (**Science**)
- Follow a compass direction to find a particular point. (**Maths**)
- Ask a group of 4–6 children to hold hands. Can they negotiate their way round a simple obstacle course whilst still holding hands? (**PE**)

Divided We Fall

BY ANTHONY McGOWAN

About this book

Cat, Ant and Tiger make a playground and discover some X-bots. Thinking that they must be friendly like Rover, Tiger approaches them but they try to steal his watch. Max comes to the rescue in the micro-buggy and, with a bit of teamwork, they manage to escape.

You will need

- *Adventure playground plan 1* Photocopy Master 62, *Teaching Handbook* for Year 2/P3
- *Adventure playground plan 2* Photocopy Master 63, *Teaching Handbook* for Year 2/P3

	Literacy Framework objective	Target and assessment focus
Speaking, listening, group interaction and drama	○ Listen to each other's views and preferences, agree the next steps to take and identify contributions by each group member **3.3**	○ We can listen to other's points of view about characters and come to a decision about whether we agree or not **AF3**
Reading See also continuous reading objectives listed on page 9.	○ Give some reasons why things happen or characters change **7.2** ○ Use syntax and context to build their store of vocabulary when reading **7.4**	○ We can explain and find the part in the story where characters change **AF2/3** ○ We can decode words using knowledge of phonics **AF1**

Before reading

To activate prior knowledge and encourage prediction

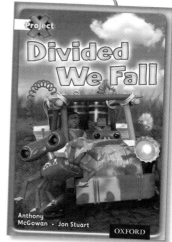

- Look at the title 'Divided We Fall'. Ask children if they understand what this means. Explain that it comes from a famous phrase 'United we stand, divided we fall'. Discuss what this might mean to the characters. (**predicting**)

- What jobs can the children think of that are better done if people work together as a team? What happens if someone helps you? (**activating prior knowledge, questioning**)

To preview the text

- Take a picture walk up to Chapter 5. What can the children deduce about the story line? How do they think the theme of teamwork might be important to the story? (**deducing, predicting**)

To support decoding and introduce new vocabulary

- Show the children some of the challenge vocabulary from this book (see the vocabulary chart on page 10), e.g. sponge (p.12), furious (p.14), sarcastically (p.6), pincers (p.25). Help them decode the words and use syntax and context to work out their meaning.

· ·>

Assessment point

Have children been able to use context and syntax to guess the meaning of unfamiliar words? AF1

To engage readers and support fluent reading

- Allocate parts to the children: the narrator, Max, Cat, Ant and Tiger. Ask them to read pages 4–9 in role using expression to show the feelings of each character.

Chapter 1 – A clean start

The micro-friends were in Max's garden. Rover, Ant's pet robot, was there, too. They were all supposed to be cleaning the micro-buggy. The buggy had been through lots of adventures with the children and it was very dirty.

"Do we really have to do this?" Tiger complained. "It's boring."

"The wheels are all clogged up," said Max, seriously. "We've got to keep the buggy in tip-top order. We don't want it to break down and leave us stranded somewhere, do we? It won't take long if we all work together."

 **During reading**

- Ask children to read Chapters 2–5.

- If you have not already done so, ask the children what to do if they encounter a difficult word, modelling with an example from the book if necessary. Remind them of the more challenging vocabulary which you looked at before reading the book.

......................................>

> ### Assessment point
>
> Listen to individual children reading and make ongoing assessments on their approaches to tackling new words and their reading fluency. **AF1**

- As they read ask them to think about what the chapter title 'Rebellion' means.

- Ask the children to consider the relationships between the characters as they read and write notes.

After reading

Returning to the text

- Recap what has happened so far. Why do the children think Max was not sure whether Tiger falling in the barrel was an accident or not?

- Why do they think Max gave Tiger the dirtiest job. Was this a deliberate act? (**questioning, deducing, drawing conclusions**)

- Ask them to find the page in the story where Max feels sorry for treating his friends the way he did. (page 19)

Building comprehension

- Ask the children to discuss how they feel about the relationships between the four characters. Ask half the group to consider these chapters from Max's point of view and the other half to consider them from Tiger's point of view. Encourage children to decide who they empathize with more. (**personal response, empathizing**).

· ·>

- As a group, read Chapter 6. Four children could take the part of the characters and another one or two the narrator.

- Can the children tell you on which page Max apologizes for shouting to his friends? (page 31). Why do the children think he did this? What does he do that shows he is trying to make amends? (**deducing, inferring**)

· ·>

- Place children in groups of three: one child will be an interviewer and the other two will take on the role of Max and Tiger. Ask the interviewer to ask each of the other characters to talk about their behaviour and actions in the story. (**deducing**, **inferring**, **drawing conclusions**)
- Ask the children to consider who the robots are. Where have they come from? Can children think of questions they would like to ask the robots? (**questioning**)

Building fluency

- Allow children some time to practise rereading Chapter 5, ensuring that they use the voice and vary the pace to build excitement and tension.

Follow-up activities

Writing activities

- Write their own version of Chapter 5. (**longer writing task**)
- Write their own version of the next book in the series entitled 'The Truth about X-bots'. (**longer writing task**)
- Create a poster to advertise a car-washing company. (**short writing task**)

Cross-curricular and thematic opportunities

- Ask groups of children to work as a team to design an adventure playground (using the *Adventure playground 1* Photocopy Master) and then make a miniature one. Ask them to use *Adventure playground 2* to evaluate how successfully they followed their plan. (**DT**)
- Investigate measurements and scale for making an adventure playground. (**Maths**)
- Solve multiplication problems related to the X-bots, e.g. if there were 4 times as many X-bots how many would there be? (**Maths**)

Let's Form a Band

BY HAYDN MIDDLETON

About this book

This non-fiction text looks at how bands, particularly pop and rock bands, are formed. It explores the role of each musician in a band and describes other people who are involved in helping the band, such as sound engineers and roadies.

You will need

- *Band helpers* Photocopy Master 64, *Teaching Handbook* for Year 2/P3
- *Wanted!* Photocopy Master 65, *Teaching Handbook* for Year 2/P3
- Short clips of a variety of music, especially different band music

	Literacy Framework objective	Target and assessment focus
Speaking, listening, group interaction and drama	○ Speak with clarity and use appropriate intonation when reading and reciting texts 1.1	○ We can read our books clearly and use the tone of our voice to keep people interested **AF1**
Reading See also continuous reading objectives listed on page 9.	○ Use syntax and context to build their store of vocabulary when reading 7.4 ○ Draw together ideas and information from across a whole text, using simple signposts in the texts 7.1	○ We can decode words using knowledge of phonics **AF1** ○ We can explore the book and interpret the information we find **AF2/3**

Before reading

To activate prior knowledge and encourage prediction

- Talk to the children about music that they like to listen to. Discuss current bands and pop-stars. Talk to the children about different styles of music. Have they ever heard of jazz or reggae, etc.? Take time to listen to some snippets of music and discuss children's personal responses to what they hear. (**activating prior knowledge**)

- Talk to the children about why teamwork might be important in a band. Do any of the children play an instrument? Perhaps they might like to play it to the rest of the group.

To support decoding and introduce new vocabulary

- You may wish to point out some of the high or medium frequency words or practise decoding some of the words in this book and listed in the vocabulary chart on page 11.

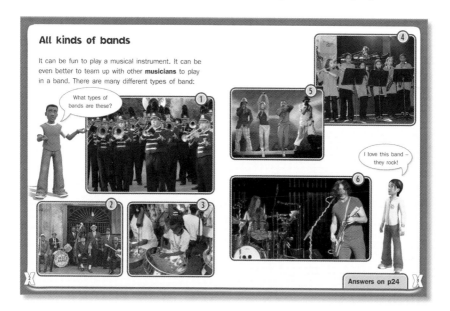

All kinds of bands

It can be fun to play a musical instrument. It can be even better to team up with other **musicians** to play in a band. There are many different types of band:

What types of bands are these?

I love this band – they rock!

Answers on p24

To engage readers and support fluent reading

● Look through the rest of the pictures in the book. Are there
any people the children recognize? Try to name as many
people or groups as possible so that the terms become
familiar to the children when they come to read the book.
Allow children time to discuss the different bands and to
become motivated about the subject. (**activating prior
knowledge, previewing**)

 During reading

● Ask the children to read to the end of page 16.

● If you have not already done so, ask the
children what to do if they encounter a
difficult word, modelling with an example
from the book if necessary, e.g. *guitarist* (p.4),
rhythm (p.5). Remind them of the more
challenging vocabulary which you looked at
before reading the book.

· ·➔

Assessment point

Listen to individual
children reading and
make ongoing
assessments on their
approaches to tackling
new words and their
reading fluency. AF1

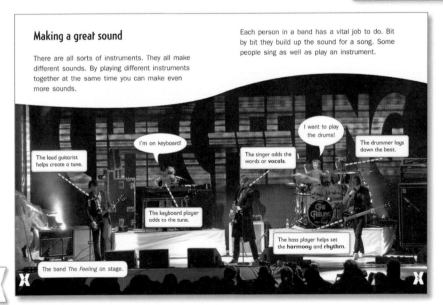

Making a great sound

There are all sorts of instruments. They all make
different sounds. By playing different instruments
together at the same time you can make even
more sounds.

Each person in a band has a vital job to do. Bit
by bit they build up the sound for a song. Some
people sing as well as play an instrument.

I'm on keyboard!

I want to play
the drums!

The lead guitarist
helps create a tune.

The singer adds the
words or **vocals**.

The drummer lays
down the beat.

The keyboard player
adds to the tune.

The bass player helps set
the **harmony** and **rhythm**.

The band *The Feeling* on stage.

 **After reading**

Returning to the text

- Ask the children about the different bands they found out about. What have they discovered that they did not know already? (**recall**, **summarising**, **synthesizing**)
- Ask the children:
  - Have you ever downloaded music from the Internet?
  - Why do children think the Arctic Monkeys gave away free CDs?
  - How has the Internet made it easier for bands to become famous?
  - What are the different ways you can create a band? Which do you feel is the best way? Why? (**questioning**)

$\cdots\cdots\cdots\cdots\cdots\cdots\cdots\cdots\cdots\cdots\cdots\cdots\rightarrow$

> **Assessment point**
>
> Can children explore and interpret the information they have read? AF2/3

Building comprehension

- Ask the children why they think *Take That* split up and then got back together. (**recall**, **deducing**, **inferring**, **drawing conclusions**)
- Look at the pictures on pages 20 and 21. Discuss how each band's outfit creates a certain image. (**deducing**, **inferring**, **drawing conclusions**)
- Which outfits do the children like best? Encourage them to express their personal preferences, giving reasons why. (**personal response**)
- Ask the children what they felt about this book. Did they like the subject matter? Was it interesting to read? How well was the book presented? (**personal response**)

Building fluency

- Ask children to choose a section to reread to the rest of the group. Give them time to practise the section and explain that you would like to hear them read clearly, using their voice to keep their audience interested.

Assessment point

Can children read their sections clearly and use the tone of their voice to keep people interested? AF1

. . . . >

Follow-up activities

Writing activities

- Children could write a fact file on their favourite band. (**short writing task**)
- Write song lyrics to raise money for a charity. (**longer writing task**)
- Complete a book review about this book and display it in the book corner for others to read. (**longer writing task**)
- Give out the *Band helpers* Photocopy Master and ask the children to write notes about the different roles of people who help a band. (**short writing task**)
- Design an advert to advertise for a new band member. Children could use the *Wanted!* Photocopy Master to help them plan their advertisement. (**short writing task**)

Cross-curricular and thematic opportunities

- Make some musical instruments. (**Music, DT**)
- Use the made instruments to play in a group, orchestra or ensemble. (**Music**)
- Explore the different sections of an orchestra that make up its whole sound. (**Music**)
- Carry out role play auditions for a band. (**Music**)
- Create and record simple sound tracks. (**Music, ICT**)
- Design a costume or outfit for a band. (**Art**)

Fee Fie Fo... MUM!

BY SÎAN LEWIS

About this book

Sam and Samantha are twins who don't get on. Mum has had enough of their fighting and sends them to the local youth centre to attend a drama workshop. Together the quarrelling children play the part of a two-headed giant in *Jack and the Beanstalk* perfectly, and show that even people who don't get on can still work together as a team!

You will need

- *Emotions* Photocopy Master 66, *Teaching Handbook* for Year 2/P3
- *Playscript* Photocopy Master 67, *Teaching Handbook* for Year 2/P3

	Literacy Framework objective	Target and assessment focus
Speaking, listening, group interaction and drama	○ Consider how mood and atmosphere are created in live or recorded performance 4.3	○ We can produce a soundtrack to reflect atmosphere in a story **AF2/3**
Reading See also continuous reading objectives listed on page 9.	○ Give some reasons why things happen or characters change 7.2 ○ Explore how particular words are used, including words and expressions with similar meanings 7.5	○ We can plot a character's emotions and see how they change **AF3** ○ We understand how words, such as onomatopoeia, help to create atmosphere in a story **AF5**

Before reading

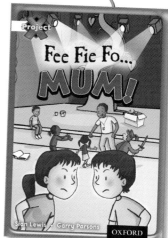

To activate prior knowledge and encourage prediction

- Focus on the front cover and look at the title. Ask the children what other story this reminds them of. What is different about this title? (It uses the word *Mum* instead of *Fum*). (**activating prior knowledge**)

To preview the text

- Take a picture walk through the text and ask children to deduce what is going to happen in the story using only the pictures as clues. (**previewing**)

- Can the children spot something else that is different about this story from the original? (The giant is a two-headed giant.) Ask children to pose questions about this, considering the theme of 'Working as a Team'. Why might a two-headed giant be in a story about team work? (**deducing, predicting**)

To support decoding and introduce new vocabulary

- You may wish to point out some of the high or medium frequency words or practise decoding some of the words in this book and listed in the vocabulary chart on page 11.

To engage readers and support fluent reading.

- Read Chapter 1 to the children. Model how to read with expression.

During reading

- Ask the children to read Chapters 2 and 3.
- Ask children to choose a character (Sam or Samantha). As they read, ask them to think about how their character is feeling and how their emotions change.
- If you have not already done so, ask the children what to do if they encounter a difficult word, modelling with an example from the book if necessary. Remind them of the more challenging vocabulary which you looked at before reading the book.

· ·>

> **Assessment point**
>
> Listen to individual children reading and make ongoing assessments on their approaches to tackling new words and their reading fluency. **AF1**

 After reading

Returning to the text

- Ask the children:
  - Why do you think Mum wrote a note to the twins instead of telling them about the drama class?
  - How do you think Mum was feeling at this point (when she wrote the note). Have you ever driven your parents or carers to these emotions?
  - How do the twins feel? (**questioning**)
- Can the children predict what might happen at the end of the story? (**predicting**)

Building vocabulary

- Discuss the onomatopoeic words on pages 5 and 6 and how they add to the feeling of chaos during breakfast.

· ·>

> **Assessment point**
>
> Do children see why the author has chosen onomatopoeic words to create a certain atmosphere in the story? **AF5**

Building comprehension

- Give out the *Emotions* Photocopy Master and allocate a character to a pair of children: Sam, Samantha and Mum. Ask the children to fill in the graph for the chapters they have read, by drawing emoticons, e.g. happy face, sad face, angry face, etc. to show how their character is feeling at various points. Start by asking the children to draw an emoticon for their character up to 'Reading the playscript' on their graph. (**deducing**, **inferring**, **drawing conclusions**)

  ·>

- Create a soundtrack for the story using body percussion for pages 5, 12 and 29. Use this to help children to determine the atmosphere of the story at these points. (**visualizing and other sensory experiences**)

  ·>

- Children can independently read the rest of the story. Ask children to complete their *Emotions* graph and continue to plot how each of the characters is feeling in Chapters 4 and 5. How do they think the children feel when everyone laughs at them? (**deducing**, **inferring**, **drawing conclusions**)

  ·>

Assessment point

Have the children been able to plot how their character is feeling at this stage of the story? AF3

Assessment point

Can children create a soundtrack to reflect the atmosphere in a story? AF2/3

Assessment point

Can children correctly deduce the emotions of the characters? AF3

Follow-up activities

Writing activities

- Write posters to promote the play in the story. (**short writing task**)
- Children create their own section of the play, inserting the scene of the arguing two-headed giant on the *Playscript* Photocopy Master. (**longer writing task**)
- Children could attempt to write their own playscript for a different fairy tale. (**longer writing task**)

Other literacy activities

- After writing their playscript (see Writing activities), children could present their play to an audience. (**speaking and listening**)
- Read the story of *Jack and the Beanstalk* and compare it with other fairy tales.

Cross-curricular and thematic opportunities

- Play team-building games to encourage children to work together, e.g. blindfold one child while another child guides him or her round a safe area; make body sculptures of different structures, e.g. a rocket. (**PE**)
- Make miniature play-sets in shoe boxes to use in their own plays. (**DT**)
- Make animated movies for a play. (**ICT**)

The Beautiful Team

BY HAYDN MIDDLETON

About this book

This report – which includes chronological and non-chronological features – shows how World Cup winners Brazil, known as 'The Beautiful Team', are a great example of how team members work hard together to win.

You will need

- *The Beautiful Team* summary Photocopy Master 68, *Teaching Handbook* for Year 2/P3
- *Newspaper report* Photocopy Master 69, *Teaching Handbook* for Year 2/P3

	Literacy Framework objective	Target and assessment focus
Speaking, listening, group interaction and drama	○ Explain ideas and processes using imaginative and adventurous vocabulary and non-verbal gestures to support communication 1.3	○ We can describe events using exciting vocabulary **AF2**
Reading See also continuous reading objectives listed on page 9.	○ Explain organizational features of text, including alphabetical order, layout, diagrams, captions, hyperlinks and bullet points 7.3 ○ Use syntax and context to build their store of vocabulary when reading 7.4	○ We can point out and describe some presentational features and differences between texts **AF4** ○ We can decode words using knowledge of phonics **AF1**

Before reading

To activate prior knowledge and encourage prediction

● Focus on the title of the book 'The Beautiful Team'. What do children understand by this term? Try to clarify any misconceptions they may have. (**activating prior knowledge**)

● How many children are a member of a sports team? What is it like being part of a team? How do they feel when they are successful? What does it feel like to lose?

● What do the children know about football? Do they have a favourite team? (**activating prior knowledge**)

To preview the text

● Take a picture walk through the book. Can children deduce what team this book is about? Can they work out why they might be called the beautiful team? (**previewing**)

To support decoding and introduce new vocabulary

ⓐ **Phonic opportunity** Focus on some of the challenging names in this book. Work with children to use phonic knowledge to decode them, e.g. breaking words down into syllables (*czech/o/slo/vakia*).

● You may also wish to point out some of the high or medium frequency words or practise decoding some of the words in this book and listed in the vocabulary chart on page 11.

To engage readers and support fluent reading

● Read pages 2 and 5 to the children, modelling how to use your voice expressively. As you read the last paragraph of page 3 encourage children to use their knowledge from the picture walk to predict what team the book might be about. (**predicting**)

During reading

- Ask pairs of children to select a section to read and to become experts on it.
- As they read ask them to notice information about why Brazil might be called 'The Beautiful Team'.
- If you have not already done so, ask the children what to do if they encounter a difficult word, modelling with an example from the book if necessary.
  Remind them of the more challenging vocabulary which you looked at before reading the book.

· ·>

Assessment point

Listen to individual children reading and make ongoing assessments on their approaches to tackling new words and their reading fluency. AF1

After reading

Returning to the text

- Go around the group, asking pairs of children:
  - What have you discovered about the Brazilian football team?
  - Who was Brazil's star player?
  - What can children recall about Pele? (**questioning**)
  - What different ways has the author used to present information in their section? Draw children's attention to the list and use of bullet points in particular. Discuss why these presentational devices may have been selected by the author. (**deducing, inferring, drawing conclusions**)

· ·>

Assessment point

Can children identify different presentational devices and discuss why the author might have selected them to present the information? AF4

Organizing the team

Great teams do a lot of work in between games. They don't just play together, they **train** together too. Then they plan exactly how to play their next match.

Players at great club teams like Liverpool train and plan together all through the season. They live close together so it is easy to keep meeting up. This makes the team strong.

Brazil's players play for club teams all over the world. That means they can't meet up often for training and for team talks. When they *do* meet up, Brazil's coach has to organize his team fast. He has to let all the players know exactly what jobs they must do in the games.

Brazil's coach, Dunga, talks to his players before an important training session.

Brazil's coach in 1958 was Vicente Feola. He sometimes seemed to fall asleep during games but he had done *his* job already – by organizing the team.

Building comprehension

- Give out *The Beautiful Team summary* Photocopy Master and ask the children, in pairs, to make notes about the key information their section. (**recall**, **summarizing**, **determining importance**)
- Children could read the rest of the book independently and note down on their summary sheets the key information.

Building fluency

- Talk about how vocabulary can be used to make events sound exciting. Work as a group to collect vocabulary to help describe the football game. Ask children to try to create an oral football commentary for the football match described. (**other sensory responses**)

··>

Assessment point

Can children use vocabulary to describe events and make them sound interesting? **AF2**

Follow-up activities

Writing activities

- Write the 'ingredients' for a good team. (**shorter writing task**)
- Write a newspaper report about a sports match, using the frame on the *Newspaper report* Photocopy Master. (**longer writing task**)

Cross-curricular and thematic opportunities

- Put together a minimum of four teams (football or a different sport) and create a tournament. (**PE**)
- Create and interpret charts showing winning teams/league tables/points gained, such as school sports day charts, Olympic teams medal charts and football charts. (**Maths**)
- Locate Brazil on a world map. (**Geography**)
- Investigate and locate other countries that have won the World Cup (on page 4) on a map. (**Geography**)